M000194708

BOOK ANALYSIS

By Georgina Murphy

The Sun Also Rises

by Ernest Hemingway

Bright
≡Summaries.com

ERNEST HEMINGWAY

AMERICAN WRITER

- **Born in Illinois in 1899.**
- **Died in Idaho in 1961.**
- **Notable works:**
  - *A Farewell to Arms* (1929), early Modernist novel
  - *For Whom the Bell Tolls* (1940), war novel
  - *The Complete Short Stories of Ernest Hemingway* (1987), posthumous collection

Ernest Hemingway is regarded as one of the first, most influential American Modernists. Between 1920 and the mid-1950s, he published seven novels, six short story collections and two works of non-fiction. Hemingway won the Pulitzer Prize in 1953 for his last major work of fiction, *The Old Man and the Sea* (1952), and in 1954 he was awarded the Nobel Prize for Literature.

Hemingway is remembered for developing the 'iceberg theory', an economical, minimalist style alternatively known as the 'theory of omission'.

As he writes in *Death in the Afternoon* (1932), "the dignity of movement of an iceberg is due to only one-eighth of it being above water" (1999: 154). By focusing on surface elements of the story (just "one-eighth"), Hemingway believed that the underlying significance of the narrative could shine through more poignantly and powerfully, despite not being obviously referred to. As Hemingway's iceberg style aims to capture the truth, his novels are considered to be works of realism. Thematically, Hemingway often uses a setting of conflict to examine human love, lust, fear, loss, guilt and betrayal.

FIESTA: THE SUN ALSO RISES

EARLY MODERNIST NOVEL

- **Genre:** novel
- **Reference edition:** Hemingway, E. (2004) *Fiesta: The Sun Also Rises*. London: Arrow Books.
- **1st edition:** 1926
- **Themes:** love, conflict, realism, masculinity, anti-Semitism, women, power

Fiesta: The Sun Also Rises (published as *The Sun Also Rises* in the United States and *Fiesta* in England) is a novel about a group of American and British expatriates living in Paris after World War One. We follow the story of an American journalist named Jake Barnes, who is in love with a divorced British woman named Lady Brett Ashley. Brett and Jake agree that although they are in love, they cannot be together. Through Jake, we are also introduced to his friend Robert Cohn, an American writer, Brett's fiancé Mike

Campbell and Bill Gordon. The main action of the novel occurs when the party decides to go away to Spain in order to go fishing and to watch the Pamplona bull-running fiesta. Whilst in Spain, Brett becomes the object of Cohn's unreciprocated obsession, as she starts an affair with a 19-year-old bullfighter named Pedro Romero. As new romances blossom, Jake is forced to accept that he will never be happily with the woman he loves. In this way, Hemingway's novel examines how lonely, lovesick individuals search for a meaningful place within a post-war world.

SUMMARY

BOOK ONE: JAKE'S OLD ROMANCE

The novel opens with the narrator, Jake Barnes, describing his friend Robert Cohn, a former middleweight boxing champion of Princeton University. Jake admits that he is not particularly impressed by Cohn's achievement, and suggests that he is quite a forgettable person. As such, Jake is surprised when Cohn's former boxing coach, Spider Kelly, "not only remembered Cohn" but also "wondered what had become of him" (p. 4). The reader also learns that Cohn is Jewish and, due to anti-Semitism whilst at Princeton, turned to boxing out of "bitter[ness]" (*ibid*.). Cohn married young, endured an unhappy five-year marriage, had three children and was then left by his wife. After the divorce, he moved to California and started working for a magazine, through which he met a woman called Frances. Cohn and Frances now live in Paris, where Cohn starts writing poor novels. Jake is Cohn's "tennis friend" and Braddocks is his "literary friend"

(p. 5). We learn that Frances is very controlling and possessive of Cohn; however, when Cohn travels to New York to get his book published, Jake reckons "that was where Frances lost him" (p. 7). One day after Cohn's return to Paris, he interrupts Jake at work and asks him to come on a trip to South America, but Jake refuses. Despite the fact that Jake is working, he goes for a mid-day drink with Cohn, who again tries to convince him to go to South America. Jake is unable to get rid of Cohn, so the pair head back up to the office and Cohn falls asleep.

That night, Jake goes for a solo drink at the Napolitain, where he makes eye contact with a girl who then joins him. Jake comments, "with her mouth closed she was a rather pretty girl" (p. 13). They go to dinner, and the reader learns her name is Georgette and that Jake is American. Jake complains that he is sick because he was injured in the war. Seeing his friends in the other room, Jake temporarily leaves the conversation to go and see Braddocks, Cohn, Frances, Mrs Braddocks and others. After dinner, Jake and Georgette join the party to go dancing. Brett then arrives at the club, and Cohn is infatuated with her. Jake and Brett leave the club together in a taxi, and Brett confides that she has been miserable. Jake and Brett kiss, and the reader learns that they are in love with one another; however, they are adamant that they cannot be together. Hemingway does not specify exactly why this is, but suggestively implies that it is because of Jake's war wound. They take the taxi to Café Select for some more drinks, but Jake soon leaves to go home. Before he leaves, they arrange to meet at five o'clock at the Crillon the next day. Jake is kept awake by memories of the war, and then thoughts about Brett. Later that night, he wakes up to a noisy commotion between Brett and the building's concierge. Jake lets a very drunk Brett upstairs to his flat, where they have a drink. Soon after, Brett leaves.

The next morning, Jake finds Cohn waiting for him at work. They go for lunch, and Cohn asks Jake about Brett. Jake tells him that Brett is getting a divorce and is going to marry a man named Mike Campbell. We learn that Jake and Brett met when she was working as a Voluntary Aid Detachment nurse in a hospital during the war. Cohn seems overly interested in Brett, despite the fact that he does not really know her. At five o'clock, Jake heads to the Crillon to wait for Brett, who does not turn up. He therefore goes to Café Select, where he meets a friend called Harvey Stone. Harvey tells him that he has not eaten for five days because he has no money. Cohn then turns up, and Harvey insults him and leaves. Addressing the reader directly, Jake remarks that he has "not shown Robert Cohn clearly" (p. 39), and reveals that before falling for Brett he had a nice, sweet, albeit slightly boring, nature. Frances then shows up and asks to speak with Jake in private. She thinks that Cohn is going to leave her. Jake does not understand why Cohn does not stand up for himself when Frances verbally attacks him. When he returns to his flat, Brett and Count Mippipopolous turn up. Brett and Jake talk about their love for one another, and she reveals that she is going on a trip to San Sebastian. Later, they have dinner and go dancing. They talk about Brett's engagement to Mike, and Brett admits that she never thinks about him.

BOOK TWO: BULLFIGHTING AND BUST-UPS

At the start of book two, we learn that Cohn is out of the country and Frances has left for England. Jake enjoys not having Cohn around. Jake's friend Bill Gorton arrives from America, and the two plan to go on a fishing trip to Spain and to go to the Pamplona bull-running festival. While they are out, they run into Brett, who tells them she has just returned. Once introductions have been made, Jake and Bill leave to go and eat, and later meet up with Brett and Mike. Mike gets very drunk, and Bill and Jake leave to go and watch a fight. The next morning, Jake receives a letter from Cohn, who says that he is still in Spain. Jake replies, saying that he and Bill will leave Paris on the 25th and will meet him in Bayonne. That evening, Mike and Brett ask if they can also join on the trip. When Mike leaves, Brett reveals that she spent her time in San Sebastian with Cohn.

The next morning, Bill and Jake head to Spain by train. Arriving in Bayonne, they meet Cohn, who says he has read all of Bill's books. They then get in a car to go to Spain, and stop in a town for the food. Jake notes that Cohn appears nervous as he does not know whether Bill and Jake know he was in San Sebastian with Brett. During dinner, Jake and Cohn leave for the train station to see if Mike and Brett have arrived, but find that they do not show up. Returning to the restaurant, Jake receives a telegram from Brett saying that she and Mike have stopped for the night in San Sebastian. Jake makes Cohn jealous by not showing him the telegram. Jake buys their bus tickets to Burgete, where they are going fishing; however, Cohn decides to go and meet Mike and Brett in San Sebastian instead. Bill and Jake then make their way to Burgete, where they spend five days fishing, during which Jake admits to Bill that he has been in love with Brett for years.

One morning, Jake receives a letter from Mike saying that they will meet them in Pamplona on Wednesday, which happens to be the same day Jake receives the letter. They also receive a telegram from Cohn saying that he will be there too. Bill and Jake therefore make their way to Pamplona. We learn that Jake is "an aficionado" – someone who is "passionate about the bullfights" (p. 115). They find Brett, Mike and

Cohn at a café. They then go and see the bulls being unloaded: they are clearly very dangerous. Back at the café, Mike gets drunk and starts accusing Cohn of obsessing over Brett, mocking him by saying "don't you know when you're not wanted?" (p. 124).

On July 6th the festival begins, and the town explodes with drinking, partying and bullfighting. After some heavy drinking, Cohn passes out in the back of a shop, but wakes up in time for dinner. After dinner, Jake passes out in Cohn's room and is then woken up at 6am by the sound of bulls being released through the town. Jake watches from his balcony, while the others later return home and sleep until noon. That afternoon, they go and watch a bullfight. The fight they watch on the second day, however, is "much better" (p. 145), mainly because they are so impressed by the performance of a very young and good-looking bullfighter named Romero. Jake realises that Brett is particularly intrigued by him, as she insists on having a closer view during his next fight.

A few days later, Jake's party are dining in a café and see Romero. Jake goes to speak to Romero, and we learn that he was born in Ronda and started bullfighting three years ago in Malaga. Brett asks Jake to introduce her and their friends to Romero. Once Romero leaves, Mike takes another opportunity to verbally attack Cohn. Later that evening, Brett and Jake go for a walk to have a chat. Brett asks Jake if he still loves her, to which he says yes. Brett then tells Jake that she is in love with Romero and asks for Jake's help in finding him. They find him in a café, and Jake leaves them to flirt. Jake then goes to find Bill and Mike and Cohn shows up, demanding to know where Brett is. When Jake refuses to tell him, Cohn knocks both Mike and Jake out. Somewhat recovered, Jake goes back to the hotel, where he finds Cohn crying and begging for forgiveness. Jake forgives him, and Cohn tells him that he is going to leave in the morning. The next morning, Jake learns that Cohn beat up Romero, who is now being cared for by Brett.

On the final day of the fiesta, Brett, Jake and Bill go to the bullfight where Romero is fighting. Romero kills both of his bulls and is praised for his talent. That night, Jake goes to see Mike, who tells him that Brett has left town with Romero:

now that there are just three of them left – Mike, Jake and Bill – "it seemed as though about six people were missing" (p. 195).

BOOK THREE: A BLEAK CONCLUSION

The fiesta draws to a close, and Mike, Bill and Jake rent a car to drive out of Spain. Jake decides to stay in San Sebastian for a week, while Mike goes to Saint Jean de Luz and Bill heads back to Paris. Whilst in San Sebastian, Jake receives a telegram from Brett asking him to come to Madrid, as she is "rather in trouble" (p. 209). Jake leaves straight away, and finds Brett in a hotel. She says that she has broken up with Romero and plans to go back to Mike. She is in a very emotional place – " I could feel her crying. Shaking and crying" (p. 213) – and Jake attempts to comfort her. As they travel through the Spanish city in a taxi, Brett mourns the "damned good time" they could have had together, to which Jake responds "isn't it pretty to think so?" (p. 216): the novel therefore ends with Jake's realisation that he can never be with the woman he loves.

CHARACTER STUDY

JAKE BARNES

Jake is the protagonist and narrator of *Fiesta: The Sun Also Rises*. Hemingway does not give us a physical description of Jake, focusing instead on his reflections, experiences and inner psychology. Similarly, although we know that Jake is American, we do not find out very much about his childhood or young adulthood; his past is therefore deliberately mysterious. Despite this, Hemingway makes it clear that Jake's experience as a soldier in World War I has had a profound effect on him, and suggests that his injuries have left him unable to have sex. For example, when Jake meets Georgette, "she looked up to be kissed. She touched me with one hand and I put her hand away" (p. 13). Rejecting her sexual advances, Jake excuses himself as being "sick" (*ibid*.), but later says that he "got hurt in the war" (p. 14); as such, Hemingway implies that this war wound has left him impotent. This is confirmed through Jake and Brett's first one-on-one conversation, where Jake says, "what happened to me is supposed to be funny", and Brett admits "I laughed about it too, myself, once" (p. 23). Yet their attempt to make light of the situation is undercut by Jake's awareness of the fact that "certain injuries or imperfections are a subject of merriment while remaining quite serious for the person possessing them" (*ibid.*). As such, Hemingway implies that Jake's impotence means that he can never be with Brett, and "there's not a damn thing [they] could do" (*ibid.*) to change it. Jake has been left mentally and physically scarred by the war, and thus represents the 'Lost Generation': broken survivors who are 'lost' in the sense that they are wandering and direction-less in the aftermath of World War I.

Meanwhile, Hemingway makes it clear that Jake understands the dilemma of the 'Lost Generation' and seeks to separate himself from it. As such, Jake finds a sense of purpose through his passion for nature, fishing and bullfighting. During Bill and Jake's fishing trip, nature takes on a restorative, healing function, as is made clear through Bill's mock-sermon:

"Let no man be ashamed to kneel here in the great out-of-doors. Remember the woods were God's first temples. Let us kneel and say: "Don't eat that, Lady – that's Mencken"". (p. 106)

Although this episode is purposefully funny, Bill and Jake's appreciation of the "great out-of-doors" strikes a semi-religious, healing note, and serves as a much-needed escape from the directionless nature of the Lost Generation. Similarly, Jake's passion for bullfighting means that he can connect with like-minded people through their shared "aficion": "there was no password, no set questions that could bring it out, rather it was a sort of oral spiritual examination" (p. 115). Again, Hemingway uses religious terms to describe Jake's escape from the post-war world, suggesting that his passions are both restorative and curative. Jake therefore seems acutely aware of the dilemma of the Lost Generation: as he tells Cohn at the beginning of the novel, "you can't get away from yourself by moving from one place to another" (p. 10).

The fact that Jake and Brett will never be together tinges their love with an underlying pain. They clearly care for each other deeply; for example, when Jake suggests that they had "better keep away from each other", Brett insists, "I have to see you" (p. 23). However, whilst Brett's commitment to Jake fluctuates, Hemingway makes it clear that Jake is unconditionally in love with her. He is even willing to introduce Brett to Romero after she admits that she is "mad about the Romero boy", thinking that she is "in love with him" (p. 159). Even though hearing Brett speak about Romero in this way is clearly very painful for Jake, he still agrees to introduce her to him, and thus puts her happiness above his own. Furthermore, when, at the end of the novel, Brett sends for Jake's help from Milan, he instantly goes to meet her, although his bitterness is apparent: "Send a girl off with one man. Introduce her to another to go off with him. Now go and bring her back. And sign the wire with love" (p. 210). Resigned to the fact that he will always be her source of support, Jake's commitment to Brett is clear.

LADY BRETT ASHLEY

Brett is the object of Jake, Mike, Cohn and Romero's interest in the novel. We are first introduced to her through Jake's eyes, where he describes her as "damned good-looking", with hair "brushed back like a boy's", and "built with curves like the hull of a racing yacht" (p. 19). Like Jake and the other men in the novel, she spends a lot of time drinking, dancing and partying. Hemingway plays into rather stereotypical representations of women by suggesting that she is a dangerous seductress, with the ability to corrupt the men around her. Jake tells the reader that "before [Cohn] fell in love with Brett" he was "nice", "kept in shape" and had a "funny sort of undergraduate quality about [him]" (p. 39). As such, Jake implies that Brett is the cause of Cohn's decline, and his changed nature makes other men dislike him, as well as causing Cohn to attack Jake, Mike and Romero. Furthermore, Mike scorns that Cohn "calls [Brett] Circe" and "claims that she turns men into swine" (p. 125). Hemingway's reference to 'Circe' here alludes to the seductress of Homer's *Odyssey*, who transformed men into pigs. In this way, by suggesting that Brett's independence and sexual freedom is to blame for male corruption, Hemingway engages with a very misogynistic and stereotypical presentation of women.

Meanwhile, Hemingway also gives voice to Brett's vulnerability and inner psychology, thus departing from mere two-dimensional stereotypes. She frequently confides in Jake about how "miserable" (p. 21) she is, which breaks down her confident and assured exterior. Furthermore, Hemingway suggests that she wanders aimlessly between different relationships in an attempt to find purpose in her life: she is divorced, due to marry Mike, has an affair with Cohn, starts a relationship with Romero, and is denied the future she wants with Jake. Her search for meaning in an unstable post-war world is therefore reflective of the wanderings of the Lost Generation: she is clearly just as unfulfilled and unhappy as the men she surrounds herself with.

ROBERT COHN

Cohn is the first character we meet in the novel, and through Jake's narrative voice we find out about his past – from his school years, to his failed marriage, to his career as a writer. We find out that he is from one of the "richest Jewish families in New York" (p. 4) and did not fight during the war. We learn that he experienced anti-Semitism during his days at college, and turned to boxing in order to combat his "painful self-consciousness" (*ibid.*). It is evident that the group that Cohn travels with to the fiesta persistently attack his insecurities: for example, Mike mocks his shyness, saying, "Do say something. Don't just sit there" (p. 123), and warns Brett to "expect trouble" if she goes "about with Jews" (p. 176). Furthermore, Cohn is shunned for behaving differently to the other men, with Mike sneering "Why don't you ever get drunk, Robert?" (p. 124), and mocking him for not enjoying the bullfighting: "You mustn't get bored at your first bullfight, Robert" (p. 144). Jake's mistreatment of Cohn is similarly rooted in anti-Semitism, and as Ernest Lockridge writes, "anti-Semitism [...] is the deepest flaw in the novel's narrator, the flaw upon which his jealous hatred is predicated" (Hays, 2011: 196). With this in mind, it becomes clear that whilst Cohn's lust and desire for Brett is hardly different from that of Jake, Mike and Romero, he receives a much greater backlash to it due to their ingrained anti-Semitic values.

ANALYSIS

NARRATIVE POINT OF VIEW

The Sun Also Rises is written from Jake's narrative perspective. This means that the reader receives a subjective story that is filtered through Jake's point of view, and only has access to the events that he experiences. As such, the reader is left with narrative gaps. For example, we do not find out precisely what happened when Brett and Cohn spent a trip together in San Sebastian, but only find out snippets of second-hand accounts. Similarly, we only gain a vague idea of how Brett and Romero's relationship came to an end, as Brett repeatedly insists "let's not talk about it" (p. 212). Furthermore, our perception of the other characters is dependent on Jake's – he even admits near the beginning of the novel that he feels he has "not shown Robert Cohn clearly" (p. 39). The reader therefore ought to be wary of taking Jake's perception of the other characters in the novel as the objective truth. For example, on the first page of the novel Jake notes that a boxing injury "certainly improved [Cohn's] nose" (p. 3): here, Jake's description of Cohn is clearly influenced by Jewish stereotypes, meaning that his narrative is tainted by ingrained prejudice. As such, in order to gain greater clarity with regard to characters and events, the reader needs to look past Jake's subjective narrative voice.

CONTRIBUTION TO MODERNISM

Generally speaking, the Modernist period spans from the early 20th century to around 1960, and is regarded as radical, unconventional and experimental in style, form and thinking. The Modernist movement was born out of the effects of World War One, during a time of global instability, conflict and violence, and the literature of this period consequently reflects the struggle to find meaning in a radically unstable world. Hemingway has come to be classified as part of a group of American writers known as the 'Lost Generation': survivors who were 'lost' in the sense that they were wandering and directionless in the aftermath of WW1. By exploring the psychological complexities of both Jake and Brett, *The Sun Also Rises* encapsulates the deep uncertainty of purpose and meaning in an unstable world that is so common within early Modernist works.

Hemingway's innovative use of the iceberg theory is regarded as a huge contribution to Modernism. Hemingway gives the reader a very concise, stripped-back narrative that only scratches the surface of what he is trying to communicate. The rest of Hemingway's meaning, in all its ambiguity, is hidden beneath the words on the page; his style therefore serves as a way of capturing the chaos of the times in which he lived. Hemingway's theory of omission is well illustrated at the very end of the novel:

> "'Oh, Jake,' Brett said, 'we could have had such a damned good time together.' Ahead was a mounted policeman in khaki directing traffic. He raised his baton. The car slowed suddenly pressing Brett against me. 'Yes.' I said. 'Isn't it pretty to think so?'" (p. 216)

Within a few short lines, Hemingway communicates both Brett and Jake's lament of what they could have had, had circumstances been different. Meanwhile, Jake's slightly cynical, bitter response "Isn't it pretty to think so?" illustrates how their dream of a relationship will never be more than an unfulfilled fantasy. Furthermore, by breaking up the dialogue with a description of the policeman and the slowing car, Hemingway slows the pace of this episode to create a bleak, dejected tone. Yet the fact that the "car slowed suddenly" also creates an image of the vehicle rapidly changing speed, which seems to contrast with the languid pace of their conversation. As such, Hemingway underscores this slow, dejected pace with an image of rapid change, suggesting that despite Jake's apparent acceptance that their relationship has no future, he is perhaps more shocked than he lets on. Hemingway's carefully selected images and dialogue therefore serve as a way of hinting at the very complex and ambiguous emotions that lie beneath the surface.

MASCULINITY

Hemingway explores the concept of insecure masculinity within *Fiesta: The Sun Also Rises*. Most notably, Jake feels significantly less masculine because the war has left him impotent. As such, the way the war has destroyed his ideals of masculinity reflects how pre-war values have been shaken by the horrors of war, thus leaving the post-war reality uncertain and insecure. Jake's own insecurity is reflected through the way his impotence is thought of as a fate worse than death. He recalls the colonel's visit to him in hospital says, when the colonel said, "'you [...] have given more than your life'" (p. 27). Although Jake sarcastically reflects "What a speech! I would like to have it illuminated to hang in the office." (*ibid.*), it is clear he is deeply insecure about his inability to have sex, and what it means for his masculinity. As such, Romero, as a seemingly courageous, stoic and competent individual, has often been interpreted as a symbol of ideal masculinity.

It therefore seems that Jake criticises what he perceives as the 'unmanly' men around him in order to cope with his own insecure masculinity. For example, Cohn is also repeatedly mocked for his 'unmanly' behaviour: Mike compares him to a castrated bull, saying, "I would have thought you'd love being a steer, Robert" because "they lead such a quiet life" and "never say anything"

(p. 123). As Cohn does not subscribe to the masculine of ideals of self-assurance and confidence, his quietness is thus aligned with weakened masculinity. Jake's homophobia further confirms his sense of insecurity. When Brett arrives at a bar in Paris with a group of gay men, Jake comments, "they always made me angry" and wishes to "swing on one, anyone" (p. 17). Furthermore, he mocks "the tall blond youth['s]" effeminacy, describing with scorn how he "danced big-hippily" (*ibid.*). As such, Jake disparages these men as a group of "superior, simpering" (*ibid.*) outsiders and cannot accept them as men, viewing them instead as an example of weakened masculinity. Hemingway therefore suggests that for Jake to move away from the idea that he is a damaged man and thus adapt to the post-war world, he must overcome stereotypical representations of masculinity.

FURTHER REFLECTION

SOME QUESTIONS TO THINK ABOUT...

- What do you think about the presentation of women in the novel?
- To what extent do you feel sympathy for Cohn? Justify your answer.
- Compare Cohn's values of love and chivalry with those of the other men in the novel.
- How does Hemingway present Mike and Romero in the novel?
- Why do you think Hemingway chooses bullfighting as a backdrop to his novel?
- What is the significance of Catholicism in the novel?
- In 2000, the novel was adapted into a one-act opera. How successfully do you think *Fiesta: The Sun Also Rises* might translate to this medium?
- How does Hemingway present the passage of time in the novel?

We want to hear from you!
Leave a comment on your online library
and share your favourite books on social media!

FURTHER READING

REFERENCE EDITION

- Hemingway, E. (2004) *Fiesta: The Sun Also Rises*. London: Arrow Books.

REFERENCE STUDIES

- Hays, P. L. (2011) *The Critical Reception of Hemingway's* The Sun Also Rises. New York: Camden House.

- Hemingway, E. (1999) *Death in the Afternoon*. New York: Scribner Classics.

- Parrish, T. (2013) *The Cambridge Companion to American Novelists*. Cambridge: Cambridge University Press.

ADDITIONAL SOURCES

- Dearborn, M.V. (2017) *Ernest Hemingway: A Biography*. London: Penguin Random House.

ADAPTATIONS

- *Fiesta*. (2013) [Play]. Alex Helfrecht. Dir. London: Trafalgar Studios.
- *The Sun Also Rises*. (2000) [Opera]. Adapted by Webster A. Young. New York: Long Island Opera Company.
- *The Sun Also Rises*. (1984) [Film]. James Goldstone. Dir. USA: NBC.
- *The Sun Also Rises*. (1957) [Film]. Henry King. Dir. USA: 20th Century Fox.

MORE FROM BRIGHTSUMMARIES.COM

- Reading guide – *A Farewell to Arms* by Ernest Hemingway.
- Reading guide – *A Moveable Feast* by Ernest Hemingway.
- Reading guide – *For Whom the Bell Tolls* by Ernest Hemingway.
- Reading guide – *The Old Man and the Sea* by Ernest Hemingway.

www.brightsummaries.com

Ebook EAN: 9782808013185

Paperback EAN: 9782808013192

Legal Deposit: D/2018/12603/417

Cover: © Primento

Digital conception by Primento, the digital partner of publishers.

Made in the USA
Middletown, DE
28 July 2019